LANDMARK TOP TENS

The World's Most Amazing
National Parks

Ann Weil

Raintree

Chicago, Illinois

www.heinemannraintree.com
Visit our website to find out more information about Heinemann-Raintree books.

To order:
☎ Phone 888-454-2279
💻 Visit www.heinemannraintree.com to browse our catalog and order online.

© 2012 Raintree
an imprint of Capstone Global Library, LLC
Chicago, Illinois

Customer Service: 888-454-2279
Visit our website at www.heinemannraintree.com

Edited by Megan Cotugno and Vaarunika Dharmapala
Designed by Victoria Allen
Picture research by Hannah Taylor and Ruth Blair
Illustrated by HL Studios and Oxford Designers
    and Illustrators
Original illustrations © Capstone Global Library Ltd (2011)
Production by Camilla Crask
Originated by Capstone Global Library Ltd
Printed and bound in the United States of America,
North Mankato, MN
15 14 13 12 11
10 9 8 7 6 5 4 3 2

Library of Congress Cataloging-in-Publication Data
Weil, Ann.
    The world's most amazing national parks / Ann Weil.—1st ed.
       p. cm.—(Landmark top tens)
    Includes bibliographical references and index.
    ISBN 978-1-4109-4243-2 (hc)—ISBN 978-1-4109-4254-8
    (pb) 1. National parks and reserves—Juvenile literature. 2.
    Natural areas—Juvenile literature. I. Title.
    SB481.3.W45 2012
    333.78'3—dc22   2010038409

092011
006318RP

Acknowledgments
The author and publishers are grateful to the following for permission to reproduce copyright material: Alamy Images pp. 5 (© Philip Scalia), 16 (© Prisma/Heeb Christian), 17 (© Prisma Bildagentur AG); Corbis pp. 12 (epa/Jon Hrusa), 15 (Frans Lanting), 18 (© Stephen Frink), 22 (Magnus Elander), 7; © Dina Pinos p. 20 top; Photolibrary pp. 4 (age fotostock/Terrance Klassen), 8 (age fotostock/Gonzalo Azumendi), 9 (Picture Press/Sven-Erik Arr); 19 (Waterframe Images/Tom Stack), 25 (age fotostock/Javier Larrea), 27 (Ambient Images/Peter Bennett), 11; Shutterstock pp. 6 (© Lee Prince), 13 (© Stuart Taylor), 14 (© rebvt), 20 bottom (© worldswildlifewonders), 21 (© Tony Horthrup), 23 (© Chris Howey), 24 (© Rafa Irusta), 26 (© Villiers Steyn).

Cover photograph of Uluru-Kata Tjuta National Park, Australia reproduced with permission of Corbis (Paul Souders).

We would like to thank Daniel Block for his invaluable help in the preparation of this book.

Every effort has been made to contact copyright holders of material reproduced in this book. Any omissions will be rectified in subsequent printings if notice is given to the publisher.

Disclaimer
All the internet addresses (URLs) given in this book were valid at the time of going to press. However, due to the dynamic nature of the internet, some addresses may have changed, or sites may have changed or ceased to exist since publication. While the author and publisher regret any inconvenience this may cause readers, no responsibility for any such changes can be accepted by either the author or the publisher.

Contents

National Parks 4

Yellowstone National Park... 6

Sarek National Park.. 8

Uluru-Kata Tjuta National Park...................................... 10

Kruger National Park 12

Galapagos National Park... 14

Yasuni National Park... 16

Biscayne National Park 18

Arenal Volcano National Park..20

Northeast Greenland National Park............................22

Vatnajökull National Park...24

National Parks in Danger 26

National Parks Facts and Figures 28

Glossary..30

Find Out More..31

Index...32

Some words are printed in bold, **like this**. You can find out what they mean in the glossary.

National Parks

A national park is public land for everyone to visit and enjoy. Governments all over the world have chosen some incredible places to support and protect as national parks.

The waterfall at Iguazu National Park in Argentina is amazing. At certain times of the year, more water flows through here than any other waterfall in the world. Iguazu means "Great Waters."

A new idea

Long ago there were no national parks. Over time more and more land became private. Millions of people lived and worked in cities. For many, getting back to nature meant visiting a park.

There are about 7,000 national parks throughout the world. Most protect natural settings along with the plants and animals that live there. Some national parks are **urban**.

A national park in the city of Lowell, Massachusetts, shows visitors how water power helped shape the **Industrial Revolution**.

Yellowstone National Park

Yellowstone was the world's first national park. Other protected areas existed, but this was the first time a national government took responsibility for a park. Yellowstone was home to Native Americans long before it became a park. From around 11,000 years ago, people lived and hunted there. The park is famous for its **geysers**, hot springs, and amazing rock formations.

There are more than 300 geysers in the park. The most famous is "Old Faithful." It erupts about 20 times a day.

Yellowstone National Park

Location: Wyoming, USA

Size: 3,472 square miles (8,992 square kilometers)

That's Amazing!

Yellowstone National Park spans three U.S. states: Wyoming, Montana, and Idaho.

John Muir was born in Dunbar, Scotland. He moved to the United States in 1849.

An active park

This amazing park includes an active volcano. There are about 1,000–3,000 earthquakes there each year! The park also includes one of the world's largest **petrified** forests.

John Muir

John Muir (1838–1914) was one of the first **environmentalists**. He persuaded President Theodore Roosevelt to preserve more land in the United States for future generations to enjoy.

Sarek National Park

In 1909 Sweden became the first European country to have a national park. Little has changed in the park since then. There are no places for people to stay overnight. Hiking and camping are allowed. But a visit to this remote park is risky. There are avalanches and heavy snowstorms in winter. In summer, heavy rain can cause **flash floods**.

Sarek National Park
Location: Lapland, Sweden
Size: 746 square miles
(1,931 square kilometers)
That's Amazing!
Sarek is one of the nine original national parks of Sweden.

The spectacular scenery in Sarek National Park includes ice-covered mountains and the Rapa River **delta**.

Elks such as this one live in Sarek. Elks have big appetites. During the winter, an adult elk can eat 5,000 pine trees!

Peaks and Animals

The park includes 100 **glaciers** and six of Sweden's highest peaks. It is home to large elks, bears, wolverines, lynx, and many smaller animals.

Wilderness

Wilderness means a place that is in its natural state. The lack of shelter and facilities make wilderness parks challenging to visit. But for those with the right equipment and experience, wilderness parks offer a rare opportunity to see nature as it was before humans changed the land.

Uluru-Kata Tjuta National Park

This park uses the **Aboriginal** names for two natural features in Australia: Uluru (Ayers Rock) and Kata Tjuta (Mount Olga). Both are the visible tips of a huge underground rock formation that was once deep underwater. The Anangu people are the traditional owners of the land. The Aboriginal name of Uluru has been used since 1993.

This national park is located close to the actual center of Australia. Like most of Australia, it has a desert climate.

Ancient Seabed

This park was once part of an ancient seabed. The sea disappeared about 300 million years ago.

A sacred place

Uluru (Ayers Rock) is 1,141 feet (348 meters) high—as tall as a 95-story building! Many tourists visit the park to climb to the top of the rock. But the path crosses places that are **sacred** to the Aboriginal people. There is a sign at the park asking visitors to respect the Aboriginal culture and view the rock from below.

The iron inside the rock rusts at the surface. This gives Uluru its unusual glowing red color.

Uluru-Kata Tjuta National Park

Location: Australia

Size: 512 square miles (1,362 square kilometers)

That's Amazing!

The image of Uluru is a national symbol for Australia.

Kruger National Park

Kruger is one of the oldest and largest national parks in Africa. The original **reserve** was established in 1898 to protect Africa's unique wildlife from hunters, **poachers**, and cattle farmers. It was expanded in 1926. Today Kruger covers a huge area that includes protected sections on public and private land. There are no fences, so animals can move freely from one park to another.

Unfortunately, even elephants that live in parks are not safe. Experts think that as many as 38,000 elephants were killed by poachers in 2006.

The "Big Five"

Elephants are the biggest of the "Big Five" animals people can see on safari. The others are lions, rhinos, buffalo, and leopards. Parks such as Kruger help to protect these and other amazing wild animal species from becoming **extinct**.

Kruger National Park

Location: South Africa

Size: Approximately 7,722 square miles (20,000 square kilometers)

That's Amazing!

Park visitors can get up-close views of wild animals in their natural surroundings.

Visitors to Kruger usually see four of the "Big Five" animals on safari. The hardest to spot are leopards. These wild cats are **nocturnal**.

Galapagos National Park

The Galapagos Islands are home to unusual animals that live nowhere else on Earth. Some animals that used to live there are now **extinct**. Even more species, including the Galapagos giant tortoise, would now be extinct were it not for **conservationists**.

Galapagos National Park

Location: Pacific Ocean off the coast of Ecuador on the Equator

Size: 2,678 square miles (6,936 square kilometers)

That's Amazing!

In 1959, the government of Ecuador made 90 percent of the Galapagos Islands a national park.

The blue-footed booby is one of many amazing animals found on the Galapagos Islands.

Charles Darwin

Charles Darwin's visit to the Galapagos Islands in 1835 changed the history of science. "It seems to be a little world within itself," he wrote. The plants and animals Darwin saw there helped him form the **theory of evolution**. Darwin did not like the Galapagos at first. The black sand on the beach burned his feet—even through his shoes!

Naming the Galapagos

An early explorer reported seeing giant tortoises on the islands. Their shells looked like horse saddles. *Galapagos* is Spanish for "saddles."

The Galapagos giant tortoise is the largest living tortoise.

Yasuni National Park

Yasuni National Park is in the Amazon rain forest. Rain forests are famous for having high numbers of plants and animals. Yasuni sets world records for **biodiversity** for an area of its size. For example, just a few acres of land contains as many as 100,000 insect species. That's the greatest species diversity in the world!

National parks like Yasuni are even more important now since logging (cutting down trees) is destroying more rain forests.

This golden-mantled tamarin is one of the amazing creatures found in Yasuni National Park.

Saving a park

Protecting the plants and animals in this amazing national park may also help save a traditional way of life for some of the last **indigenous** people still living in the Amazon.

Yasuni National Park

Location: Ecuador

Size: Approximately 6,500 square miles (16,835 square kilometers)

That's Amazing!

This park has world record numbers of many kinds of plants and animals.

Biscayne National Park

Biscayne is one of the largest marine national parks in the United States. Ninety-five percent of this park, close to Miami in Florida, is underwater. The park includes part of Biscayne Bay, which has the third-largest coral reef in the world. It also includes the northernmost islands of the Florida **Keys**.

Biscayne National Park
Location: Florida, USA
Size: 270 square miles (700 square kilometers)
That's Amazing!
There are 72 shipwrecks in the park. Visitors to the park can dive or snorkel around six of these historic sites.

Coral reefs are home to many amazing plants and animals. Eighty percent of the world's **biodiversity** lives in the ocean.

The roots of mangrove trees hold the coastline together and provide homes for many different animals.

UNITED STATES

GULF OF MEXICO

MEXICO

N

FLORIDA

Miami •

Biscayne Bay

Biscayne National Park

Key
⚓ Shipwrecks

FLORIDA KEYS

0   50 miles

0   50 kilometers

BioBlitz!

In 2010 there was a "BioBlitz" at Biscayne National Park. More than 2,500 people, from scientists to students, listed all the different kinds of plants and animals they saw in the park during a 24-hour period.

Arenal Volcano National Park

Arenal Volcano National Park in Costa Rica was established in 1995. It is part of a much larger conservation area, and includes several different habitats. This increases its **biodiversity**. About half of all land-dwelling **vertebrates** (birds, mammals, reptiles, and **amphibians**) known in Costa Rica can be found in the park.

"Zipline" tours through the forest canopy draw more tourists to Costa Rica's national parks.

Costa Rica's rain forests are home to many animals, including monkeys and this rare, beautiful bird called the Quetzal, which was **sacred** to the ancient people of Central America.

Costa Rica has more than 200 volcanoes. Arenal is considered one of the top 10 most active volcanoes in the world.

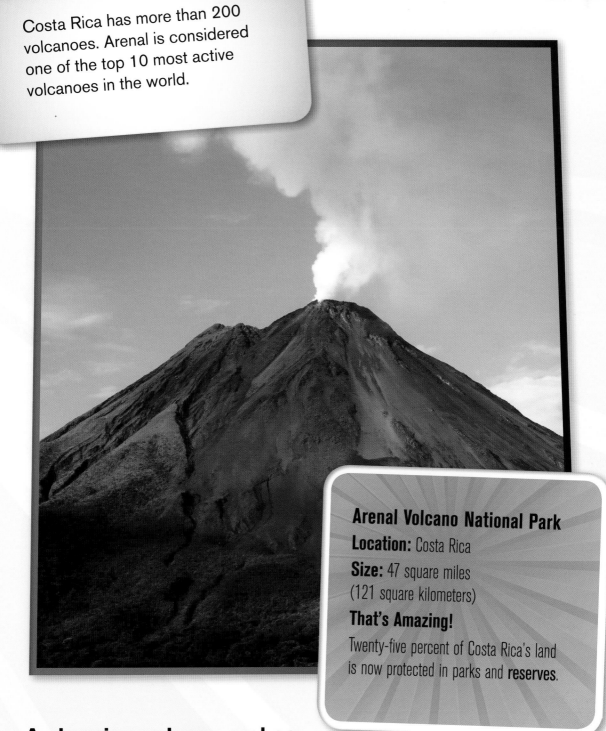

Arenal Volcano National Park
Location: Costa Rica
Size: 47 square miles
(121 square kilometers)
That's Amazing!
Twenty-five percent of Costa Rica's land is now protected in parks and **reserves**.

A sleeping volcano wakes

Arenal volcano was "sleeping" for 400 years before a sudden and deadly eruption in 1968. Giant rocks, lava, and ash buried three villages, and 87 people were killed. Today visitors to this park can see scars on the land from that eruption.

Northeast Greenland National Park

Greenland is the largest island in the world. It is also home to the largest national park in the world: Northeast Greenland National Park. About one-third of the island is protected. That's an area bigger than the state of Texas! But there are not many tourists. A few people go to study the weather and protect the land and animals. **Inuit** people are allowed to hunt seals and whales.

Cruises bring visitors to see the polar bears and giant walruses that live and hunt in the park.

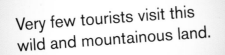

Very few tourists visit this wild and mountainous land.

Peary Land

The park includes Peary Land. This amazing part of the park is the northernmost ice-free area in the world. It was named after the Arctic explorer Robert Peary (1856–1920). Peary led a North Pole expedition in 1909.

Northeast Greenland National Park

Location: Greenland (Danish territory)

Size: 375,291 square miles (972,000 square kilometers)

That's Amazing!

This park covers one-third of the largest island on Earth!

Vatnajökull National Park

The largest national park in Europe is also one of the newest. Vatnajökull National Park covers about 12 percent of the surface of Iceland. It was officially created on June 7, 2008, and brings together areas that used to be separate national parks.

Dettifoss waterfall in Vatnajökull National Park is the largest in Europe.

Vatnajökull National Park

Location: Iceland

Size: 4,633 square miles (12,000 square kilometers)

That's Amazing!

This amazing park has Iceland's highest mountain, largest glacier, and Europe's most powerful waterfall!

A glacier is a river of ice that moves slowly down a mountain.

Glaciers

It takes a very long time for **glaciers** to form. First, snow piles up on a mountain. It must be cold enough so that the snow never melts. As more snow falls, its weight pushes down and compresses the bottom layer into blue glacial ice. Eventually this glacial ice starts to move under the pressure of its own weight. Many natural features we see in landscapes today were shaped by moving glaciers.

National Parks in Danger

National parks are in danger for many reasons. South African national parks are losing more and more rhinos to **poachers**. Poachers kill the animals to get their horns, which sell for a lot of money. People in Asia use the horns to make special medicines.

In 2009 poachers killed 122 rhinos in South African national parks, and that number continues to rise.

Uncontrolled wildfires endanger parks and people. Wildfires can be caused by lightning strikes, or by accidents—or on purpose.

Other Dangers

Invasive plants could destroy the **biodiversity** at Point Reyes National Park in California. Invasive plants are nonnative species that use resources that native plants need in order to survive.

Pollution and global warming

Oil spills, such as the one in the Gulf of Mexico in 2010, destroy wildlife habitats. Biscayne National Park escaped the worst of this spill, but it may not be so lucky in the future. **Global warming** is also melting **glaciers** all over the world, including those in national parks.

National Parks Facts and Figures

Many countries all over the world have national parks. National parks are special places maintained by a nation's government for everyone to enjoy. Some national parks are home to unusual animals and plants. Which national park do you think is the most amazing?

Yellowstone National Park

Location: Wyoming, USA

Size: 3,472 square miles (8,992 square kilometers)

That's Amazing!

Yellowstone National Park spans three U.S. states: Wyoming, Montana, and Idaho.

Sarek National Park

Location: Lapland, Sweden

Size: 746 square miles (1,931 square kilometers)

That's Amazing!

Sarek is one of the nine original national parks of Sweden.

Uluru-Kata Tjuta National Park

Location: Australia

Size: 512 square miles (1,362 square kilometers)

That's Amazing!

The image of Uluru is a national symbol for Australia.

Kruger National Park

Location: South Africa

Size: Approximately 7,722 square miles (20,000 square kilometers)

That's Amazing!

Park visitors can get close-up views of wild animals in their natural surroundings.

Galapagos National Park

Location: Pacific Ocean off the coast of Ecuador on the Equator

Size: 2,678 square miles (6,936 square kilometers)

That's Amazing!

In 1959, the government of Ecuador made 90 percent of the Galapagos Islands a national park.

Yasuni National Park

Location: Ecuador

Size: Approximately 6,500 square miles (16,835 square kilometers)

That's Amazing!

This park has world record numbers for many kinds of plants and animals.

Biscayne National Park

Location: Florida, USA

Size: 270 square miles (700 square kilometers)

That's Amazing!

There are 72 shipwrecks in the park. Visitors to the park can dive or snorkel around six of these historic sites.

Arenal Volcano National Park

Location: Costa Rica

Size: 47 square miles (121 square kilometers)

That's Amazing!

Twenty-five percent of Costa Rica's land is now protected in parks and **reserves**.

Northeast Greenland National Park

Location: Greenland (Danish territory)

Size: 375,291 square miles (972,000 square kilometers)

That's Amazing!

This park covers one-third of the largest island on Earth!

Vatnajökull National Park

Location: Iceland

Size: 4,633 square miles (12,000 square kilometers)

That's Amazing!

This amazing park has Iceland's highest mountain, largest **glacier**, and Europe's most powerful waterfall!

Glossary

Aboriginal the original people of Australia. Aboriginal people lived in Australia long before settlers arrived from Europe.

amphibians animals that are born in the water and live on land as adults. Frogs are amphibians.

biodiversity range or variety of animals and plants in a place

conservationist person who works to save and protect threatened places and animals

delta triangle-shaped area where sand and soil collects at the mouth of a river where the water flows into an ocean, sea, or lake

environmentalist person who works to protect the natural world

extinct animals and plants that have died out completely and no longer exist

flash flood sudden, powerful flow of water due to heavy rainfall

geyser hot spring that regularly throws a jet of hot water or steam into the air

glacier river of solid ice that moves slowly down a mountain

global warming rise in temperature of the surface of the Earth

indigenous native people who continue to live in the same area and with many of the same traditions as their ancestors

Industrial Revolution period in history (1800s to early 1900s) when there were many new discoveries and inventions

Inuit original people of Greenland

keys small, low islands of sand or coral

nocturnal active at night, such as certain animals that hunt after dark

petrified turned to stone

poacher someone who breaks the law to hunt and kill animals for money

reserve protected area of land

sacred describes something that is very important in a religion

theory of evolution an idea about how animals developed into their present form

urban to do with city life

vertebrate animal that has a backbone

Find Out More

Books

Augustin, Byron and Jake Kubena. *Yellowstone National Park*. New York, NY: Marshall Cavendish Benchmark, 2010.

Briscoe, Diana. *Jane Goodall: Finding Hope in the Wilds of Africa*. Bloomington, Minn.: Red Brick Learning, 2005.

Gallagher, Breandan and Debbie Gallagher. *Protecting Earth's History*. Mankato, Minn.: Smart Apple Media, 2011.

Woods, Michael and Mary B. Woods. *Seven Natural Wonders of North America*. Minneapolis, Minn.: Twenty-First Century Books, 2009.

Websites

http://www.factmonster.com/spot/nps1.html
Find out more about National Parks in the United States.

www.nsta.org/publications/interactive/galapagos/activities/adventuring.html
Learn more about the Galapagos Islands on this site.

http://www.world-national-parks.net/
A website with information about national parks around the world.

Index

Aboriginal people 10, 11
animals 9, 12–15, 16, 20, 22, 26
Arenal Volcano National Park 20–21
Argentina 4
Australia 10–11
Ayers Rock 10, 11

biodiversity 16, 18, 20, 27
Biscayne National Park 18–19, 27

canopy tours 20
conservationists 14
coral reefs 18, 19
Costa Rica 20–21

Darwin, Charles 15

earthquakes 7
Ecuador 16–17
environmentalists 7
extinction 13, 14

flash floods 8
Florida Keys 18, 19

Galapagos National Park 14–15
geysers 6
glaciers 9, 25, 27
global warming 27
Greenland 22–23

hot springs 6

Iceland 24–25
Iguazu National Park 4
indigenous people 17
Industrial Revolution 5
invasive plants 27

Kruger National Park 12–13

logging 16

mangrove trees 19
marine parks 18–19
Muir, John 7

Native Americans 6
Northeast Greenland National Park 22–23

Peary Land 23
petrified forest 7
poachers 12, 26
Point Reyes National Park 27
pollution 27

rain forests 16, 20
reserves 12, 21
rock formations 6, 10, 11

sacred sites 11
safaris 13
Sarek National Park 8–9
shipwrecks 18, 19
South Africa 12–13, 26
Sweden 8–9

theory of evolution 15

Uluru-Kata Tjuta National Park 10–11
urban parks 5
United States 5, 6–7, 18–19, 27

Vatnajökull National Park 24–25
volcanoes 7, 21

waterfalls 4, 24
wilderness parks 9
wildfires 27

Yasuni National Park 16–17
Yellowstone National Park 6–7